EMMANUEL JOSEPH

The Resilient Dreamer, How Nostalgia and Curiosity Guide Us Through Solitude

Copyright © 2025 by Emmanuel Joseph

All rights reserved. No part of this publication may be reproduced, stored or transmitted in any form or by any means, electronic, mechanical, photocopying, recording, scanning, or otherwise without written permission from the publisher. It is illegal to copy this book, post it to a website, or distribute it by any other means without permission.

First edition

*This book was professionally typeset on Reedsy.
Find out more at reedsy.com*

Contents

1	Chapter 1: The Loneliness Paradox	1
2	Chapter 2: Embracing the Quiet	3
3	Chapter 3: The Power of Memory	5
4	Chapter 4: The Journey Inward	7
5	Chapter 5: Finding Strength in Solitude	9
6	Chapter 6: The Art of Mindfulness	11
7	Chapter 7: The Dance of Nostalgia and Curiosity	12
8	Chapter 8: The Solitary Artist	14
9	Chapter 9: The Pursuit of Knowledge	15
10	Chapter 10: The Resilient Spirit	17
11	Chapter 11: The Alchemy of Dreams	19
12	Chapter 12: The Healing Power of Solitude	20
13	Chapter 13: The Wisdom of the Ancients	22
14	Chapter 14: The Power of Reflection	23
15	Chapter 15: The Path to Self-Discovery	25
16	Chapter 16: Embracing Change	27
17	Chapter 17: The Resilient Dreamer's Legacy	29

1

Chapter 1: The Loneliness Paradox

Solitude, often misunderstood, is not merely the absence of company but a profound journey inward. The paradox of loneliness is that while it may appear to isolate, it also provides a fertile ground for growth, self-discovery, and resilience. As modern society bombards us with incessant noise, distractions, and superficial interactions, the sanctuary of solitude offers a space to recharge and reflect. It becomes a canvas upon which our dreams and aspirations take form, unhindered by external influences or judgments.

In this chapter, we explore how the quiet moments of solitude reveal the depths of our inner worlds. Nostalgia serves as a bridge to our past, allowing us to revisit cherished memories and draw strength from them. At the same time, curiosity propels us forward, sparking new ideas and possibilities. Together, these twin forces guide us through the labyrinth of solitude, turning it into a crucible for personal growth and transformation.

Nostalgia, often viewed as a bittersweet longing for the past, has the power to anchor us in times of uncertainty. It reminds us of our roots, our experiences, and the lessons we've learned along the way. As we embrace nostalgia, we find solace in the familiarity of our memories, which provide a sense of continuity and resilience. Curiosity, on the other hand, ignites our imagination, encouraging us to explore the unknown and push the boundaries of our comfort zones. It is through this delicate balance of looking back and forging ahead that we navigate the complexities of solitude.

By understanding the nuances of loneliness and its potential for growth, we can transform our solitary moments into a source of strength and inspiration. Solitude becomes a crucible for the resilient dreamer, where nostalgia and curiosity converge to guide us on a journey of self-discovery and fulfillment.

2

Chapter 2: Embracing the Quiet

In a world that values constant connectivity and productivity, the art of embracing the quiet is often overlooked. Yet, it is in these moments of silence that we can truly hear the whispers of our innermost thoughts and desires. The quiet provides a respite from the chaos of daily life, allowing us to reconnect with ourselves and our dreams. By embracing the quiet, we create a space for introspection and self-reflection, essential components of the resilient dreamer's journey.

As we learn to appreciate the stillness, we begin to uncover the hidden treasures within our minds. Nostalgia and curiosity, once drowned out by the noise of the external world, come to the forefront, guiding us through our solitude. Nostalgia invites us to revisit the experiences that have shaped us, offering valuable insights and lessons. Curiosity, meanwhile, encourages us to ask questions, seek new knowledge, and explore uncharted territories.

The practice of mindfulness can help us cultivate a deeper appreciation for the quiet. By focusing on the present moment, we become more attuned to our thoughts, emotions, and surroundings. This heightened awareness allows us to tap into our inner reservoirs of strength and creativity, transforming solitude into a source of empowerment. As we embrace the quiet, we also develop a greater sense of patience and resilience, essential qualities for navigating the challenges of life.

Through the lens of nostalgia and curiosity, we can reframe our perception of solitude. Instead of viewing it as a state of isolation, we begin to see it as an opportunity for growth and self-discovery. By embracing the quiet, we embark on a journey of introspection and personal transformation, guided by the wisdom of our past experiences and the excitement of new possibilities.

3

Chapter 3: The Power of Memory

Memory is a powerful tool that shapes our identity and influences our perception of the world. It is through the lens of memory that we revisit the past, relive cherished moments, and draw strength from our experiences. Nostalgia, as an emotional connection to our memories, plays a crucial role in guiding us through solitude. By reflecting on the past, we gain a deeper understanding of ourselves and the journey that has brought us to the present moment.

In this chapter, we explore the ways in which memory and nostalgia can serve as sources of inspiration and resilience. Our memories hold the key to our personal narratives, reminding us of the challenges we have overcome and the dreams we have pursued. By revisiting these memories, we find motivation to continue striving towards our goals, even in the face of adversity. Nostalgia provides a sense of continuity, grounding us in our past while encouraging us to embrace the future with curiosity and optimism.

Curiosity, on the other hand, compels us to question and explore the world around us. It drives us to seek out new experiences, knowledge, and perspectives, enriching our understanding of ourselves and our place in the world. When combined with the power of memory, curiosity becomes a catalyst for growth and transformation. It encourages us to look beyond the confines of our past and envision new possibilities for the future.

By harnessing the power of memory and curiosity, we can navigate the complexities of solitude with greater resilience and clarity. Our memories serve as a source of wisdom and strength, while our curiosity propels us forward on a journey of self-discovery and personal growth. Together, these forces guide us through the labyrinth of solitude, transforming it into a crucible for the resilient dreamer.

4

Chapter 4: The Journey Inward

The journey inward is a path of self-discovery and introspection, where we explore the depths of our inner worlds and uncover the essence of who we are. It is a journey that requires courage, patience, and a willingness to confront our innermost thoughts and emotions. Solitude provides the ideal environment for this journey, offering a sanctuary for reflection and personal growth. As we embark on this journey, nostalgia and curiosity become our guiding lights, illuminating the way forward.

Nostalgia, as a connection to our past, helps us make sense of our experiences and the lessons they have taught us. It allows us to draw strength from our memories, reminding us of the challenges we have faced and the resilience we have developed. Curiosity, on the other hand, encourages us to look beyond the familiar and explore new aspects of ourselves and the world around us. It fuels our desire to learn, grow, and evolve, pushing us to expand our horizons and embrace the unknown.

As we journey inward, we come to understand the importance of self-awareness and self-acceptance. By acknowledging our strengths and weaknesses, we develop a greater sense of compassion and empathy for ourselves and others. This self-awareness also empowers us to make more informed decisions and pursue our dreams with greater clarity and purpose. The journey inward is not always easy, but it is a necessary step towards personal growth and fulfillment.

Through the lens of nostalgia and curiosity, we can navigate the complexities of our inner worlds with greater resilience and clarity. By reflecting on our past experiences and embracing the excitement of new possibilities, we transform solitude into a source of empowerment and inspiration. The journey inward becomes a path of self-discovery and transformation, guided by the wisdom of our memories and the curiosity that drives us forward.

5

Chapter 5: Finding Strength in Solitude

Solitude, often perceived as a state of isolation, can be a powerful source of strength and resilience. It provides us with the opportunity to connect with our inner selves and cultivate a deeper understanding of our thoughts, emotions, and aspirations. By embracing solitude, we create a space for introspection and self-reflection, allowing us to recharge and find clarity amidst the chaos of daily life. Nostalgia and curiosity, as guiding forces, help us navigate this journey and transform solitude into a source of empowerment.

Nostalgia, as an emotional connection to our past, reminds us of the experiences that have shaped us and the lessons we have learned. It provides a sense of continuity and grounding, allowing us to draw strength from our memories and find solace in familiar experiences. Curiosity, on the other hand, propels us forward, encouraging us to explore new ideas, seek new knowledge, and embrace new challenges. Together, these forces help us find strength in solitude and navigate the complexities of our inner worlds.

As we embrace solitude, we also develop a greater sense of self-awareness and self-acceptance. By acknowledging our strengths and weaknesses, we cultivate a deeper sense of compassion and empathy for ourselves and others. This self-awareness also empowers us to make more informed decisions and pursue our dreams with greater clarity and purpose. The practice of mindfulness can help us cultivate a deeper appreciation for solitude, allowing us to focus on the present moment and become more attuned to our thoughts, emotions, and surroundings.

Through the lens of nostalgia and curiosity, we can transform solitude into a source of strength and inspiration. By reflecting on our past experiences and embracing the excitement of new possibilities, we navigate the complexities of solitude with greater resilience and clarity. Solitude becomes a crucible for the resilient dreamer, where nostalgia and curiosity converge to guide us on a journey of self-discovery and fulfillment.

6

Chapter 6: The Art of Mindfulness

Mindfulness is the practice of being fully present in the moment, aware of our thoughts, emotions, and surroundings without judgment. It is a powerful tool for navigating the complexities of solitude, allowing us to connect with our inner selves and cultivate a deeper understanding of our experiences. By embracing mindfulness, we create a space for introspection and self-reflection, essential components of the resilient dreamer's journey. Nostalgia and curiosity, as guiding forces, help us navigate this journey with greater clarity and purpose.

Nostalgia, as an emotional connection to our past, invites us to revisit cherished memories and draw strength from our experiences. It provides a sense of continuity and grounding, reminding us of the lessons we have learned and the resilience we have developed. Curiosity, on the other hand, encourages us to explore new ideas, seek new knowledge, and embrace new challenges. Together, these forces help us cultivate mindfulness and transform solitude into a source of empowerment and inspiration.

7

Chapter 7: The Dance of Nostalgia and Curiosity

In the intricate dance of nostalgia and curiosity, we find a harmonious balance that guides us through solitude. Nostalgia, with its gentle reminders of the past, provides a sense of stability and comfort. It anchors us in our memories, allowing us to draw strength from the experiences that have shaped us. Curiosity, with its boundless enthusiasm, propels us forward, encouraging us to explore new horizons and embrace new possibilities. Together, these forces create a dynamic interplay that fuels our journey of self-discovery and growth.

As we navigate the complexities of solitude, the dance of nostalgia and curiosity becomes a powerful tool for resilience. Nostalgia invites us to reflect on our past, revisiting cherished moments and drawing inspiration from our experiences. Curiosity, on the other hand, encourages us to question the world around us, seek out new knowledge, and embrace the unknown. By engaging in this dance, we create a sense of balance and harmony that helps us navigate the challenges of life with greater clarity and purpose.

Through the lens of nostalgia and curiosity, we can transform solitude into a source of empowerment and inspiration. By reflecting on our past experiences and embracing the excitement of new possibilities, we develop a deeper understanding of ourselves and our place in the world. The dance

CHAPTER 7: THE DANCE OF NOSTALGIA AND CURIOSITY

of nostalgia and curiosity becomes a guiding force, helping us navigate the complexities of solitude with grace and resilience.

8

Chapter 8: The Solitary Artist

Art has long been a powerful medium for self-expression and introspection. For the solitary artist, the quiet moments of solitude provide a fertile ground for creativity and inspiration. By embracing solitude, artists can connect with their inner selves and explore the depths of their imagination. Nostalgia and curiosity, as guiding forces, help artists navigate this journey, turning solitude into a source of artistic inspiration and growth.

Nostalgia, as an emotional connection to the past, provides artists with a rich tapestry of memories and experiences to draw from. It invites them to revisit cherished moments and explore the emotions associated with them, turning these memories into powerful works of art. Curiosity, on the other hand, encourages artists to push the boundaries of their creativity, experimenting with new techniques, mediums, and ideas. Together, these forces help artists navigate the complexities of solitude, transforming it into a source of inspiration and artistic growth.

As we explore the world of the solitary artist, we come to understand the importance of embracing solitude as a means of self-expression and creativity. By reflecting on our past experiences and embracing the excitement of new possibilities, we can transform solitude into a source of empowerment and inspiration. The solitary artist becomes a resilient dreamer, guided by the dance of nostalgia and curiosity.

9

Chapter 9: The Pursuit of Knowledge

The pursuit of knowledge is a lifelong journey that requires curiosity, dedication, and a willingness to explore the unknown. For the resilient dreamer, solitude provides the ideal environment for this pursuit, offering a space for introspection, reflection, and growth. By embracing solitude, we can connect with our inner selves and cultivate a deeper understanding of the world around us. Nostalgia and curiosity, as guiding forces, help us navigate this journey, turning solitude into a source of knowledge and wisdom.

Nostalgia, as an emotional connection to our past, reminds us of the experiences that have shaped us and the lessons we have learned. It provides a sense of continuity and grounding, allowing us to draw strength from our memories and find solace in familiar experiences. Curiosity, on the other hand, propels us forward, encouraging us to seek out new knowledge, explore new ideas, and embrace new challenges. Together, these forces help us navigate the complexities of solitude, transforming it into a source of inspiration and growth.

As we embark on the pursuit of knowledge, we come to understand the importance of embracing solitude as a means of self-discovery and intellectual growth. By reflecting on our past experiences and embracing the excitement of new possibilities, we can cultivate a deeper appreciation for the world around us. The pursuit of knowledge becomes a journey of self-discovery, guided by the dance of nostalgia and curiosity.

10

Chapter 10: The Resilient Spirit

Resilience is the ability to adapt and thrive in the face of adversity. It is a quality that requires strength, determination, and a willingness to embrace change. For the resilient dreamer, solitude provides the ideal environment for cultivating resilience, offering a space for introspection, reflection, and growth. By embracing solitude, we can connect with our inner selves and develop a deeper understanding of our strengths and weaknesses. Nostalgia and curiosity, as guiding forces, help us navigate this journey, turning solitude into a source of resilience and empowerment.

Nostalgia, as an emotional connection to our past, reminds us of the challenges we have faced and the resilience we have developed. It provides a sense of continuity and grounding, allowing us to draw strength from our memories and find solace in familiar experiences. Curiosity, on the other hand, propels us forward, encouraging us to explore new ideas, seek new knowledge, and embrace new challenges. Together, these forces help us cultivate resilience and navigate the complexities of solitude with greater clarity and purpose.

As we embrace the resilient spirit, we come to understand the importance of self-awareness and self-acceptance. By acknowledging our strengths and weaknesses, we develop a greater sense of compassion and empathy for ourselves and others. This self-awareness also empowers us to make more informed decisions and pursue our dreams with greater clarity and purpose.

THE RESILIENT DREAMER, HOW NOSTALGIA AND CURIOSITY GUIDE US THROUGH SOLITUDE

The resilient spirit becomes a guiding force, helping us navigate the challenges of life with grace and determination.

11

Chapter 11: The Alchemy of Dreams

Dreams are a powerful source of inspiration and motivation, guiding us towards our goals and aspirations. For the resilient dreamer, solitude provides the ideal environment for nurturing and cultivating these dreams. By embracing solitude, we create a space for introspection, reflection, and growth, allowing our dreams to take shape and flourish. Nostalgia and curiosity, as guiding forces, help us navigate this journey, turning solitude into a crucible for our dreams.

Nostalgia, as an emotional connection to our past, reminds us of the dreams we have pursued and the goals we have achieved. It provides a sense of continuity and grounding, allowing us to draw strength from our memories and find solace in familiar experiences. Curiosity, on the other hand, propels us forward, encouraging us to explore new ideas, seek new knowledge, and embrace new challenges. Together, these forces help us nurture and cultivate our dreams, turning them into a source of inspiration and motivation.

As we embark on the alchemy of dreams, we come to understand the importance of embracing solitude as a means of self-discovery and personal growth. By reflecting on our past experiences and embracing the excitement of new possibilities, we can transform solitude into a source of empowerment and inspiration. The alchemy of dreams becomes a guiding force, helping us navigate the complexities of life with greater clarity and purpose.

12

Chapter 12: The Healing Power of Solitude

Solitude has a profound healing power, providing us with the opportunity to connect with our inner selves and cultivate a deeper understanding of our thoughts, emotions, and aspirations. By embracing solitude, we create a space for introspection and self-reflection, allowing us to heal and grow. Nostalgia and curiosity, as guiding forces, help us navigate this journey, turning solitude into a source of healing and empowerment.

Nostalgia, as an emotional connection to our past, reminds us of the experiences that have shaped us and the lessons we have learned. It provides a sense of continuity and grounding, allowing us to draw strength from our memories and find solace in familiar experiences. Curiosity, on the other hand, propels us forward, encouraging us to explore new ideas, seek new knowledge, and embrace new challenges. Together, these forces help us heal and navigate the complexities of solitude with greater resilience and clarity.

As we embrace the healing power of solitude, we come to understand the importance of self-awareness and self-acceptance. By acknowledging our strengths and weaknesses, we cultivate a deeper sense of compassion and empathy for ourselves and others. This self-awareness also empowers us to make more informed decisions and pursue our dreams with greater clarity

CHAPTER 12: THE HEALING POWER OF SOLITUDE

and purpose. The healing power of solitude becomes a guiding force, helping us navigate the challenges of life with grace and determination.

13

Chapter 13: The Wisdom of the Ancients

Throughout history, many great thinkers, philosophers, and sages have extolled the virtues of solitude. From the contemplative practices of ancient monks to the reflective writings of renowned philosophers, the wisdom of the ancients provides valuable insights into the power of solitude. By embracing solitude, we can connect with this timeless wisdom and cultivate a deeper understanding of ourselves and our place in the world. Nostalgia and curiosity, as guiding forces, help us navigate this journey, turning solitude into a source of wisdom and inspiration.

Nostalgia, as an emotional connection to our past, invites us to reflect on the teachings and experiences of those who have come before us. It provides a sense of continuity and grounding, allowing us to draw strength from the wisdom of the ancients and find solace in their timeless insights. Curiosity, on the other hand, encourages us to explore new ideas, seek new knowledge, and embrace new challenges. Together, these forces help us navigate the complexities of solitude, transforming it into a source of wisdom and growth.

As we explore the wisdom of the ancients, we come to understand the importance of embracing solitude as a means of self-discovery and personal growth. By reflecting on the teachings of the past and embracing the excitement of new possibilities, we can cultivate a deeper appreciation for the world around us. The wisdom of the ancients becomes a guiding force, helping us navigate the complexities of life with greater clarity and purpose.

14

Chapter 14: The Power of Reflection

Reflection is a powerful tool for self-discovery and growth, allowing us to connect with our inner selves and cultivate a deeper understanding of our experiences. By embracing solitude, we create a space for introspection and self-reflection to gain a deeper understanding of our thoughts, emotions, and aspirations. Nostalgia and curiosity, as guiding forces, help us navigate this journey, turning solitude into a source of self-discovery and growth.

Nostalgia, as an emotional connection to our past, reminds us of the experiences that have shaped us and the lessons we have learned. It provides a sense of continuity and grounding, allowing us to draw strength from our memories and find solace in familiar experiences. Curiosity, on the other hand, propels us forward, encouraging us to explore new ideas, seek new knowledge, and embrace new challenges. Together, these forces help us navigate the complexities of solitude, transforming it into a source of reflection and personal growth.

As we embrace the power of reflection, we come to understand the importance of self-awareness and self-acceptance. By acknowledging our strengths and weaknesses, we cultivate a deeper sense of compassion and empathy for ourselves and others. This self-awareness also empowers us to make more informed decisions and pursue our dreams with greater clarity and purpose. The power of reflection becomes a guiding force, helping us navigate the challenges of life with grace and determination.

15

Chapter 15: The Path to Self-Discovery

Self-discovery is a lifelong journey that requires curiosity, introspection, and a willingness to explore the depths of our inner worlds. For the resilient dreamer, solitude provides the ideal environment for this journey, offering a space for reflection and personal growth. By embracing solitude, we can connect with our inner selves and cultivate a deeper understanding of our thoughts, emotions, and aspirations. Nostalgia and curiosity, as guiding forces, help us navigate this journey, turning solitude into a path of self-discovery and transformation.

Nostalgia, as an emotional connection to our past, reminds us of the experiences that have shaped us and the lessons we have learned. It provides a sense of continuity and grounding, allowing us to draw strength from our memories and find solace in familiar experiences. Curiosity, on the other hand, propels us forward, encouraging us to explore new ideas, seek new knowledge, and embrace new challenges. Together, these forces help us navigate the complexities of solitude, transforming it into a source of self-discovery and personal growth.

As we embark on the path to self-discovery, we come to understand the importance of self-awareness and self-acceptance. By acknowledging our strengths and weaknesses, we cultivate a deeper sense of compassion and empathy for ourselves and others. This self-awareness also empowers us to make more informed decisions and pursue our dreams with greater clarity and purpose. The path to self-discovery becomes a guiding force, helping us navigate the challenges of life with grace and determination.

16

Chapter 16: Embracing Change

Change is an inevitable part of life, and learning to embrace it is essential for personal growth and resilience. For the resilient dreamer, solitude provides the ideal environment for embracing change, offering a space for reflection and adaptation. By embracing solitude, we can connect with our inner selves and cultivate a deeper understanding of our thoughts, emotions, and aspirations. Nostalgia and curiosity, as guiding forces, help us navigate this journey, turning solitude into a source of empowerment and growth.

Nostalgia, as an emotional connection to our past, reminds us of the experiences that have shaped us and the lessons we have learned. It provides a sense of continuity and grounding, allowing us to draw strength from our memories and find solace in familiar experiences. Curiosity, on the other hand, propels us forward, encouraging us to explore new ideas, seek new knowledge, and embrace new challenges. Together, these forces help us navigate the complexities of solitude, transforming it into a source of empowerment and personal growth.

As we embrace change, we come to understand the importance of flexibility and adaptability. By acknowledging our strengths and weaknesses, we develop a greater sense of resilience and determination. This adaptability also empowers us to make more informed decisions and pursue our dreams with greater clarity and purpose. Embracing change becomes a guiding force, helping us navigate the challenges of life with grace and confidence.

17

Chapter 17: The Resilient Dreamer's Legacy

The legacy of the resilient dreamer is one of strength, determination, and a deep connection to the inner self. It is a legacy built on the foundation of solitude, guided by the dance of nostalgia and curiosity. By embracing solitude, we create a space for introspection, reflection, and personal growth, allowing our dreams to take shape and flourish. Nostalgia and curiosity, as guiding forces, help us navigate this journey, turning solitude into a source of inspiration and empowerment.

Nostalgia, as an emotional connection to our past, reminds us of the experiences that have shaped us and the lessons we have learned. It provides a sense of continuity and grounding, allowing us to draw strength from our memories and find solace in familiar experiences. Curiosity, on the other hand, propels us forward, encouraging us to explore new ideas, seek new knowledge, and embrace new challenges. Together, these forces help us navigate the complexities of solitude, transforming it into a source of inspiration and growth.

As we reflect on the legacy of the resilient dreamer, we come to understand the importance of self-awareness, self-acceptance, and personal growth. By acknowledging our strengths and weaknesses, we cultivate a deeper sense of compassion and empathy for ourselves and others. This self-awareness also empowers us to make more informed decisions and pursue our dreams with greater clarity and purpose. The legacy of the resilient dreamer becomes a guiding force, helping us navigate the challenges of life with grace and determination.

The Resilient Dreamer: How Nostalgia and Curiosity Guide Us Through Solitude

Imagine a world where the quiet moments of solitude are transformed into powerful tools for self-discovery and personal growth. "The Resilient Dreamer" invites you on a journey through the labyrinth of loneliness, exploring how nostalgia and curiosity can guide us towards resilience and fulfillment.

In this profound exploration, you'll discover the paradox of loneliness and how it can serve as a crucible for growth. The book delves into the art of embracing the quiet, the power of memory, and the journey inward. Each chapter offers insights into the dance of nostalgia and curiosity, the pursuit of knowledge, and the resilient spirit.

As you navigate the pages, you'll find inspiration in the solitary artist's world, the healing power of solitude, and the wisdom of the ancients. Reflection becomes a tool for self-discovery, and the path to embracing change unfolds with grace and determination.

"The Resilient Dreamer" is more than a guide; it's a testament to the strength found in solitude and the transformative power of nostalgia and curiosity. It's a call to embrace your inner dreamer, harness the wisdom of your past, and explore the boundless possibilities of your future.

www.ingramcontent.com/pod-product-compliance
Lightning Source LLC
LaVergne TN
LVHW020739090526
838202LV00057BA/6132